THE FOOD PROCESSOR COOKBOOK

Edited by
Norma Miller

Contents

This edition first published 1979 by
Octopus Books Limited
59 Grosvenor Street, London W.1.

© 1979 Octopus Books Limited

ISBN 0 7064 1071 8

Produced and printed in Hong Kong by
Mandarin Publishers Limited
22a Westlands Road, Quarry Bay

Frontispiece: CORN AND FISH MOUSSE *(page 24),*
CELERY FRITTERS *(page 24),*
EGG AND MUSHROOM CREAM *(page 26),*
CHEESE AND CELERY DIP *(page 27)*
(Photograph: Unigate)

Weights and Measures

All measurements in this book are based on Imperial weights and measures, with American equivalents given in parenthesis.

Measurements in *weight* in the Imperial and American system are the same. Liquid measurements are different, and the following table shows the equivalents:

Liquid measurements
1 Imperial pint .... 20 fluid ounces
1 American pint .... 16 fluid ounces
1 American cup .... 8 fluid ounces

Level spoon measurements are used in all the recipes.

Spoon measurements
1 tablespoon (1T) .... 15 ml
1 teaspoon .... 5 ml

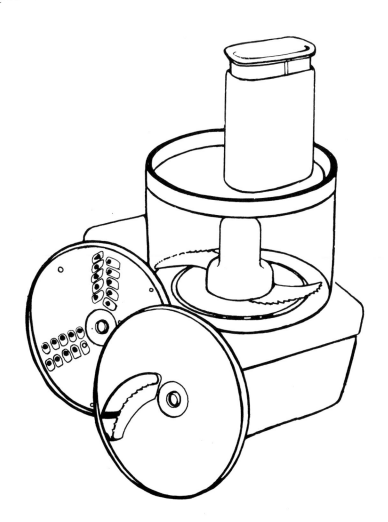

INTRODUCTION

The food processor must be the most exciting culinary aid on the market today. It really does take all the hard work out of food preparation. This versatile machine will chop, slice, grate, mince, mix, purée and blend. Whether you are someone who loves to cook, or someone who cooks because you have to, a food processor will help you prepare food in the shortest possible time, easily, efficiently, and with excellent results. Even the most inexperienced cook will find that recipes such as Vichyssoise, Beef Carbonnade, Lemon Cheesecake and Chocolate Profiteroles are well within their capabilities.

This compact, easy-to-clean machine consists of surprisingly few parts: the motor base, work bowl, work bowl cover and feed tube, food pusher, and three or four different blades. By making full use of the blades you can purée vegetables for soups, chop meat for casseroles, slice vegetables for salads, mix cake batters and pastries, knead bread and mix drinks. In seconds, all types of food can be transformed into delicious, tempting recipes to delight your family and friends.

The master tool is the metal knife which is used for all chopping. Whether you chop the food into neat, even pieces or blend it to a purée is all a matter of timing. The food processor has a very powerful motor and it will take a little time to learn exactly how long it takes to process different ingredients. It is advisable, when using the machine for the first time, to turn it on and off very quickly, checking each time to see if you have reached the right consistency. You will find you are soon able to judge the correct timing automatically.

The plastic blade is used when ingredients simply require mixing rather than chopping or processing – for example, when blending smooth sauces and dressings. The slicing disc is ideal for cutting vegetables and fruit into even slices. To use the slicing disc, you will need to cut the food to fit neatly into the feed tube. The food is then pressed down with the food pusher. A similar technique is used for the grating disc. Vegetables, fruit and cheese can be grated for use in salads, sauces and as garnishes.

It is simple to operate a food processor once you know how, but it is absolutely essential to read the manufacturer's instructions before you begin and to follow them carefully.

It makes sense to use your food processor on a regular basis and this may mean completely rethinking your whole approach to food preparation. Once you have grasped the basic technique it will be an easy step to convert your favourite recipes to this new method.

VEAL BIRDS (page 42)
(Photograph: Stork Margarine)

SOUPS

Tomato Soup

USE THE DOUBLE-BLADED CHOPPING KNIFE.

*1 lb. ripe tomatoes, skinned and
 roughly chopped
1 large onion, quartered
1 stick celery, roughly chopped
1 bay leaf
1 sprig fresh basil
2 pints (5 cups) chicken stock
 (bouillon)*

*2 tablespoons tomato purée
grated rind and juice of ¼ orange
salt and pepper
½ teaspoon sugar
chopped fresh parsley to garnish*

Place the tomatoes, onion and celery in the mixer bowl and process
until the onion is finely chopped.

   Place the tomato mixture in a large saucepan, add the herbs and
bring to the boil, stirring occasionally. Simmer for 20 minutes or
until the onion is soft. Remove and discard the herbs. Place the
cooked tomato mixture in the mixer bowl and process until smooth.
Return to the saucepan and add the chicken stock, tomato purée,
grated orange rind and juice, salt, pepper and sugar. Bring to the boil
and simmer for 10 minutes. Serve sprinkled with chopped parsley.
Serves 5-6

Almond Soup

USE THE DOUBLE-BLADED CHOPPING KNIFE.

1 pint (2½ cups) milk
1 medium onion, quartered
1 head celery, roughly chopped
4 oz. (¾ cup) blanched almonds
1 oz. (2 T) butter
1 oz. (¼ cup) plain (all-purpose)
 flour

salt and pepper
¼ pint (⅔ cup) double (heavy)
 cream
4 lemon slices, halved, to garnish

Place the milk, onion, celery, almonds, butter, flour and a little salt
and pepper in a saucepan. Bring to the boil, stirring continuously,
and simmer for 30–40 minutes or until the vegetables are tender.

Pour the soup into the mixer bowl and process until smooth.
Return to the saucepan and reheat. Taste and adjust the seasoning if
necessary. Stir in the cream, heat through but do not boil. Serve
immediately, garnished with the lemon slices.

Serves 4

Watercress and Vermicelli Soup

USE THE DOUBLE-BLADED CHOPPING KNIFE AND THE GRATING DISC
ATTACHMENT.

2 bunches watercress
2 hard-boiled eggs, quartered
2 small onions, quartered
2 pints (5 cups) chicken stock
 (bouillon)

salt and pepper
3 oz. (¾ cup) vermicelli
2 oz. (½ cup) cheese

Trim the watercress and discard any thick stalks.

Put the watercress, eggs and onions in the mixer bowl, fitted with
the double-bladed chopping knife, and process until the vegetables
are very finely chopped.

In a large saucepan mix together the chopped vegetables, chicken
stock and seasoning. Bring to the boil and simmer for 15 minutes or
until the onion is tender. Add the vermicelli and simmer for a further
2 minutes or until tender.

Process the cheese through the grating disc attachment. Sprinkle
the soup with the cheese and serve immediately.

Serves 4

Harvest Vegetable Soup

USE THE DOUBLE–BLADED CHOPPING KNIFE.

2 medium onions, quartered
3 carrots, roughly chopped
2 leeks, roughly chopped
1 clove garlic, peeled
1 ½ pints (3¾ cups) tomato juice
½ pint (1¼ cups) water
salt and pepper

⅛ teaspoon grated nutmeg
½ teaspoon dried oregano
1 oz. (2T) pearl barley
½ small cauliflower, broken into
  sprigs
4 oz. (¾ cup) sweetcorn
4 oz. (¾ cup) peas

Process 1 onion, 1 carrot, 1 leek and the garlic until finely chopped.

In a large saucepan heat together the tomato juice, water, seasoning, nutmeg and oregano. Add the processed vegetables and garlic and the remaining roughly chopped vegetables. Bring to the boil, stir in the pearl barley and simmer for 20 minutes. Add the cauliflower sprigs and simmer for a further 30 minutes or until the vegetables and the pearl barley are tender. Just before the end of the cooking time stir in the sweetcorn and peas to heat through.

Pour the soup into a warmed serving dish and serve with French bread.
Serves 4-6

Leek and Potato Soup

USE THE SLICING DISC ATTACHMENT AND THE DOUBLE–BLADED CHOPPING KNIFE.

3 medium leeks
1 large potato, roughly chopped
1 oz. (2T) butter
½ pint (1¼ cups) chicken stock
  (bouillon)

1 pint (2½ cups) milk
1 bay leaf
salt and pepper

Process the leeks through the slicing disc attachment.

Place the potato in the mixer bowl fitted with the double-bladed chopping knife. Process until the potato is finely chopped.

Melt the butter in a saucepan and add the sliced leeks and chopped potato. Cook gently for 5 minutes, stirring occasionally. Stir in the stock, milk, bay leaf and seasoning. Simmer gently for 20 minutes or until the potato is very tender. Taste and adjust the seasoning if necessary.
Serves 4

HARVEST VEGETABLE SOUP
(Photograph: Unigate)

Celery and Walnut Soup

USE THE DOUBLE-BLADED CHOPPING KNIFE.

6 sticks celery, roughly chopped
1 onion, quartered
1½ oz. (3 T) butter
2 tablespoons plain (all-purpose)
 flour
¾ pint (2 cups) milk

½ pint (1¼ cups) chicken stock
 (bouillon)
1 oz. (¼ cup) chopped walnuts
⅛ teaspoon dried thyme
salt and pepper
a sprig of parsley to garnish

Place the celery and onion in the mixer bowl and process until finely chopped.

Melt the butter in a saucepan and cook the vegetables until soft but not browned. Stir in the flour and cook for 1 minute. Gradually stir in milk and stock (bouillon) and bring to the boil, stirring continuously. Add the walnuts, thyme and seasoning and simmer for 15 minutes or until the vegetables are very soft. Serve the soup garnished with a sprig of parsley.
Serves 4

Vichyssoise

USE THE DOUBLE-BLADED CHOPPING KNIFE.

3 leeks, roughly chopped
3 potatoes, quartered
1½ oz. (3 T) butter
½ pint (1¼ cups) milk
¾ pint (2 cups) chicken stock
 (bouillon)

¼ teaspoon dried thyme
½ bay leaf
salt and pepper
Garnish:
a slice of leek, separated into rings
croûtons

Place the leeks and potatoes in the mixer bowl and process until roughly chopped. Melt the butter and fry the vegetables until soft but not browned. Add the milk, stock (bouillon), herbs and seasoning. Bring to the boil and simmer for 15 minutes or until the potato is cooked. Remove the bay leaf.

Pour the soup into the mixer bowl and process for a few seconds until smooth. Reheat the soup and serve garnished with the leek rings and croûtons.
Serves 4

Curry Soup

USE THE DOUBLE-BLADED CHOPPING KNIFE.

1 onion, quartered
1 large cooking apple, peeled and
  cored
1½ oz. (3 T) butter
1 oz. (¼ cup) plain (all-purpose)
  flour
2 teaspoons curry powder

1 pint (2½ cups) milk
½ pint (1¼ cups) beef stock
  (bouillon)
1 oz. (2 T) long-grain rice
2 tablespoons lemon juice
salt and pepper
bay leaves to garnish

Place the onion and apple in the mixer bowl and process until they
are roughly chopped.
  Melt the butter in a large saucepan and fry the onion and apple for
5 minutes. Stir in the flour and curry powder and cook for 1 minute.
Gradually stir in the milk and stock (bouillon) and bring to the boil.
Add the rice, lemon juice and seasoning and simmer for 15-20
minutes or until the rice is cooked. Serve the soup garnished with
bay leaves.
Serves 4-6

Sweetcorn Soup

USE THE DOUBLE-BLADED CHOPPING KNIFE.

1 onion, quartered
½ green pepper, seeded
1 oz. (2 T) butter
½ oz. (2 T) plain (all-purpose)
  flour
2 teaspoons paprika pepper

1 pint (2½ cups) milk
12 oz. (2¼ cups) sweetcorn kernels
salt and pepper
Garnish:
a few sweetcorn kernels
chopped fresh parsley

Place the onion and pepper in the mixer bowl and process until
roughly chopped.
  Melt the butter in a saucepan and fry the vegetables until golden
brown. Stir in the flour and paprika pepper and cook for 1 minute.
Place the vegetable mixture in the mixer bowl and, with the motor
running, pour in the milk and add the sweetcorn and seasoning and
process until smooth.
  Return the mixture to a clean saucepan, bring to the boil and
simmer for 1 minute. Serve the soup garnished with the corn kernels
and parsley.
Serves 4

Cucumber Purée Soup

USE THE DOUBLE-BLADED CHOPPING KNIFE.

1 large cucumber, roughly chopped
1 onion, quartered
2 sticks celery, roughly chopped
1 tablespoon lemon juice
½ pint (1¼ cups) chicken stock
  (bouillon)
1 oz. (2T) butter

1 oz. (¼ cup) plain (all-purpose)
  flour
½ pint (1¼ cups) milk
salt and pepper
⅛ teaspoon grated nutmeg
slices of cucumber to garnish

Place the cucumber, onion and celery in the mixer bowl and process until finely chopped. Place the vegetables in a large saucepan, add the lemon juice and stock (bouillon) and bring to the boil. Simmer for 15 minutes or until the onion is soft.

Place the butter, flour and milk in the mixer bowl and pour in the vegetable mixture. Process for a few seconds until smooth. Return to a clean saucepan, add the seasoning and nutmeg and reheat. Serve garnished with cucumber slices.
Serves 4

Shrimp Chowder

USE THE DOUBLE-BLADED CHOPPING KNIFE AND THE GRATING DISC ATTACHMENT.

1 onion, quartered
3 potatoes, quartered
½ oz. (1T) margarine
½ pint (1¼ cups) boiling water
salt and pepper

8 oz. (1 cup) peeled shrimps
¾ pint (2 cups) milk
2 oz. cheese
1 tablespoon chopped fresh parsley

Place the onion and potatoes in the mixer bowl fitted with the double-bladed chopping knife and process until finely chopped.

Melt the margarine in a saucepan and add the vegetables, water and seasoning. Bring to the boil and cook for 10 minutes or until the potato is tender. Add the shrimps and the milk and bring to the boil.

Process the cheese through the grating disc attachment. Stir the cheese and parsley into the soup and serve as soon as the cheese has melted.
Serves 4

CUCUMBER PURÉE SOUP, SHRIMP CHOWDER, CURRY
SOUP *(page 15)*, ALMOND SOUP *(page 11)*
(Photograph: Unigate)

Lobster Bisque

USE THE DOUBLE-BLADED CHOPPING KNIFE.

1 cooked hen lobster
1³/4 pints (4¼ cups) fish stock
  (bouillon)
1 small carrot, roughly chopped
1 small onion, quartered
2 oz. (¼ cup) butter
3 tablespoons flour

1 bay leaf
2 sprigs of parsley
salt and pepper
1 teaspoon lemon juice
2 fl. oz. (¼ cup) white wine
2 tablespoons cream

Crack the lobster shell and remove the meat, discarding the inedible parts. Place the lobster in the mixer bowl with half the stock (bouillon). Process until the meat is chopped. Pour into a bowl and reserve. In the mixer bowl process the carrot and onion until they are finely chopped.

In a large saucepan melt the butter, add the flour and cook, stirring, for 1 minute. Gradually add the remaining stock (bouillon), stirring continuously. Add the chopped vegetables, bay leaf, parsley, seasoning, lemon juice and wine and bring to the boil, stirring continuously. Stir in the reserved lobster mixture and any coral from the lobster shell and simmer for 3 minutes. Remove the bay leaf and parsley. Stir in the cream and serve immediately.
Serves 4-6

Cauliflower Soup

1 cauliflower, divided into florets
1 onion, quartered
1 clove garlic, peeled
1 oz. (2 T) butter
1 tablespoon flour
¾ pint (2 cups) chicken stock
  (bouillon)

¾ pint (2 cups) milk
salt and pepper
2 oz. (½ cup) button mushrooms
¼ pint (⅔ cup) single (light)
  cream
croûtons to garnish

Cook the cauliflower in boiling salted water until tender. Drain well.

Place the onion and garlic in the mixer bowl and process until very finely chopped.

Melt the butter in a saucepan, add the chopped onion and garlic and cook over a gentle heat until the onion is soft but not browned. Add the flour and mix well. Gradually add the stock and milk, stirring continuously. Add the seasoning, bring the liquid to the boil, still stirring, then cover and simmer for 15 minutes.

Place the cauliflower and mushrooms in the mixer bowl and process for a few seconds. With the motor running, gradually pour ½ pint (1¼ cups) of the sauce through the feed tube. Process until smooth. Pour into a clean saucepan and add the remaining sauce. Reheat and stir in the cream; taste and adjust the seasoning if necessary. Serve at once with croûtons.
Serves 4

Macaroni and Vegetable Soup

USE THE DOUBLE-BLADED CHOPPING KNIFE.

1 stick celery, roughly chopped
1 large leek, roughly chopped
1 medium onion, quartered
1 medium carrot, roughly chopped
1 small turnip, roughly chopped
2 slices bacon, chopped
1³/4 pints (4¼ cups) milk and
 chicken stock mixed

1 oz. (¼ cup) peas
1 oz. (¼ cup) short macaroni
salt and pepper
4 tomatoes, peeled, seeded and
 chopped

Process the celery, leek, onion, carrot and turnip until finely chopped.

Heat the bacon until the fat runs. Add the processed vegetables and cook, stirring, until well coated with the bacon fat. Add the milk and stock mixture and bring to the boil. Simmer for 20 minutes or until the vegetables are very soft. Cool slightly.

Process the vegetable mixture until smooth. Return to the pan, stir in the peas, macaroni, seasoning and tomatoes and simmer for 10 minutes or until the macaroni is tender.
Serves 4-6

MACARONI AND VEGETABLE SOUP
(Photograph: Nestlé)

APPETIZERS

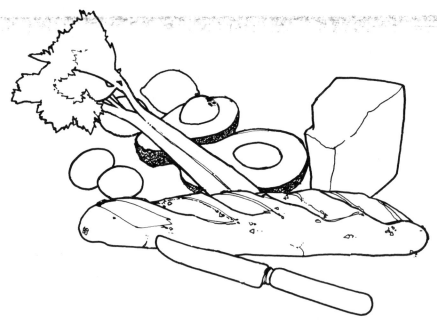

Pasta with Avocado and Lemon Sauce

USE THE DOUBLE-BLADED CHOPPING KNIFE.

8 oz. (2 cups) large pasta shells
salt and pepper
3 tablespoons olive or salad oil
1 tablespoon white wine vinegar
1 ripe avocado
grated rind and juice of 1 lemon

1 clove garlic, peeled
2 teaspoons sugar
3 tablespoons stock (bouillon)
4 spring onions (scallions), sliced
  into rings
2 tablespoons chopped fresh parsley

In a large saucepan half-filled with boiling salted water cook the pasta shells for 10-15 minutes or until just tender. Meanwhile, pour the oil, vinegar and seasoning to taste into the mixer bowl and process until mixed. Pour this dressing into a large bowl. Drain the pasta shells and while still warm toss in the oil and vinegar dressing. Leave to cool.

Halve the avocado, remove the stone (pit) and scoop out the flesh. Place the flesh, lemon rind and juice, garlic, sugar, stock, onions (scallions) and parsley in the mixer bowl and process until smooth.

Stir the avocado sauce into the pasta and spoon into a serving dish.
Serves 4

Spaghetti Carbonara

USE THE DOUBLE-BLADED CHOPPING KNIFE.

1 lb. spaghetti
8 slices lean bacon (Canadian bacon
* slices)*
2 oz. (¼ cup) butter or margarine
2 oz. (⅓ cup) peeled prawns
* (shrimp)*
2 eggs

2 egg yolks
4 tablespoons cream
salt and pepper
1 oz. Cheddar cheese
1 oz. Parmesan cheese
chopped fresh parsley to garnish

Cook the spaghetti in a large saucepan of boiling salted water for 10-12 minutes or until tender.

Place the bacon in the mixer bowl and process until roughly chopped. Fry the bacon in a pan in its own fat until crisp.

Drain the spaghetti well and place in a large bowl. Stir in the butter or margarine, the bacon and prawns (shrimp). Keep warm.

Place the eggs, egg yolks, cream, seasoning and the cheeses in the mixer bowl and process until mixed. Pour the mixture into the pan. Cook over a gentle heat, stirring continuously, until it begins to thicken and set. Pour over the spaghetti mixture and mix lightly with a fork (the heat of the dish and spaghetti should set the egg mixture a little more, bringing it to the right consistency).

Serve sprinkled with chopped parsley.
Serves 4

Stuffed Tomatoes

USE THE DOUBLE-BLADED CHOPPING KNIFE.

1 small onion, quartered
1 clove garlic, peeled
1 oz. (2 T) margarine
2 oz. (½ cup) mushrooms
2 oz. ham

1 tablespoon tomato purée
1 slice white bread, crusts removed
salt and pepper
4 large tomatoes
4 lettuce leaves to garnish

Place the onion and garlic in the mixer bowl. Process until roughly chopped. Melt the margarine in a small saucepan and fry the onion mixture for 5 minutes or until soft but not browned.

Place the mushrooms, ham, tomato purée and bread in the mixer bowl and process until they are very finely chopped. Add this mixture to the onion in the saucepan and cook for a further 5 minutes, stirring occasionally.

Cut the top off each tomato and reserve. Scoop out and discard the seeds and core and fill the cavities with the onion mixture. Replace the lids and serve on the lettuce leaves.
Serves 4

Corn and Fish Mousse

USE THE DOUBLE-BLADED CHOPPING KNIFE.

¼ pint (⅔ cup) milk
2 teaspoons cornflour (cornstarch)
2½ fl. oz. (5 T) water
½ oz. (2½ teaspoons) gelatine
¼ pint (⅔ cup) chicken stock
  (bouillon)
8 oz. (1½ cups) sweetcorn kernels,
  cooked

8 oz. (1 cup) cooked flaked cod
3 tablespoons mayonnaise
grated rind and juice of 1 lemon
salt and pepper
Garnish:
cucumber slices
watercress sprigs

Place the milk and cornflour (cornstarch) in the mixer bowl and process for a second. Pour the mixture into a saucepan and bring to the boil, stirring continuously. Cool. Pour the water into a small bowl and sprinkle over the gelatine. Stand the bowl in a saucepan of hot water and heat until the gelatine has dissolved. Stir half the gelatine mixture into the chicken stock (bouillon) and mix in the sweetcorn. Pour this mixture into a 1 pint (2½ cup) mould. Leave in a cool place to set.

In the mixer bowl place the cooled cornflour (cornstarch) mixture, remaining gelatine, flaked cod, mayonnaise, lemon rind and juice and seasoning. Process until smooth. Pour the mixture onto the sweetcorn in the mould and leave in a cool place to set. Dip the mould in hot water for a few seconds and turn out the mousse onto a chilled plate. Garnish with the cucumber and watercress.
Serves 8

Celery Fritters

USE THE DOUBLE-BLADED CHOPPING KNIFE.

4 oz. (1 cup) plain (all-purpose)
  flour
salt and pepper
¼ pint (⅔ cup) milk and water
  mixed
juice of 1 lemon

1 tablespoon corn oil
2 egg whites
3 sticks celery, cut into 1 inch
  lengths
oil for deep frying

Place the flour, seasoning, milk and water, lemon juice and oil in the mixer bowl. Process until smooth. Whisk the egg whites until stiff, add to the bowl and process for a second.

Dip the celery pieces in the batter and fry in the hot oil until golden brown. Serve with Hollandaise sauce.
Serves 4

SPAGHETTI CARBONARA (page 23)
(Photograph: John West Foods)

24

Egg and Mushroom Cream

USE THE DOUBLE–BLADED CHOPPING KNIFE.

3 oz. (³/4 cup) noodles
salt and pepper
1/2 oz. (1 T) butter
1/2 oz. (2 T) flour
1/2 pint (1 1/4 cups) milk
1 small onion, halved
1/2 teaspoon dry mustard

1/4 teaspoon mixed herbs
2 oz. (1/2 cup) button mushrooms,
 sliced
2 oz. frozen peas
2 oz. cheese
1 tomato, sliced
2 hard-boiled eggs, sliced

Cook the noodles in a large saucepan of boiling salted water for 8 minutes or until cooked. Drain well.

In the mixer bowl place the butter, flour, milk, onion, mustard and herbs and process until mixed. Pour the mixture into a saucepan and bring to the boil, stirring continuously. Add the mushrooms and peas and season to taste. Simmer for 3 minutes or until the mushrooms are cooked.

Place the cheese in the mixer bowl and process until it is finely chopped. Remove the mushroom sauce from the heat and stir in the cheese. Arrange the noodles around the edge of a warm serving dish. Pour the sauce into the centre and top with the sliced tomato and egg.

Serves 4

Taramasalata

USE THE DOUBLE-BLADED CHOPPING KNIFE.

2 slices white bread, crusts removed
milk
8 oz. smoked cod's roe, skinned
   (1 × 8 oz. jar tarama)

2 cloves garlic, peeled
¼ pint (⅔ cup) olive oil
4 tablespoons lemon juice
pepper

Soak the slices of bread in milk for 10 minutes. Squeeze out the excess milk and place in the mixer bowl together with the cod's roe (tarama) and garlic. Process until very smooth.

   With the motor switched on, pour the olive oil, a little at a time, through the feed tube until the mixture is thick and creamy. With the motor still running, add the remaining oil a little more quickly. Remove the cover, add the lemon juice and pepper and process for a second. Spoon into a serving dish and chill for 30 minutes.
Serves 6

Cheese and Celery Dip

USE THE DOUBLE-BLADED CHOPPING KNIFE.

8 oz. (1 cup) cream cheese
2 tablespoons hot milk
2 small sticks celery, roughly
   chopped

salt
⅛ teaspoon cayenne pepper
chopped chives to garnish

Place the cream cheese, hot milk, celery, salt and cayenne in the mixer bowl and process for a few seconds until smooth. Spoon the mixture into a serving dish and sprinkle with chives. Serve with crusty bread or vegetable sticks.
Serves 4

Salami Quiche

USE THE DOUBLE-BLADED CHOPPING KNIFE.

6 oz. shortcrust pastry (basic pie
  dough), see page 68
1 large onion, quartered
2 oz. cheese
4 oz. salami, sliced

2 eggs
¼ pint (⅔ cup) milk
2 tablespoons single (thin) cream
salt and pepper

Roll out the pastry and line a 7 inch fluted flan tin (pie pan).

Place the onion and cheese in the mixer bowl and process until finely chopped. Cover the base of the pastry case with the onion and cheese and the salami slices.

Place the eggs, milk, cream and seasoning in the mixer bowl and process for a second. Pour the egg mixture into the pastry case.

Bake in a moderate oven, 350°F, Gas Mark 4 for 40 minutes until the pastry is golden brown and the filling set. Serve with tomato salad.
Serves 6

Savoury Pancakes

USE THE DOUBLE-BLADED CHOPPING KNIFE.

4 oz. (1 cup) plain (all-purpose)
  flour
2 eggs
½ pint (1¼ cups) milk
¼ teaspoon salt
oil for frying
Sauce:
1 oz. (2T) butter
1 oz. (¼ cup) flour

½ pint (1¼ cups) milk
1 teaspoon mustard
salt and pepper
Filling suggestions:
8 oz. mushrooms
12 oz. cooked chicken
8 oz. cooked leeks and 4 oz. cooked
  bacon
watercress to garnish

Place the flour, eggs, milk and salt in the mixer bowl and process until the mixture is smooth. Pour the batter into a jug. Use the batter to make 8 pancakes. Keep warm.

To make the sauce, place the butter, flour, milk, mustard, seasoning and one of the suggested fillings in the mixer bowl and process until mixed. Pour the sauce into a saucepan and, stirring continuously, bring to the boil. Simmer for 5 minutes. Use the sauce to fill the pancakes, roll up and serve immediately, garnished with watercress.
Serves 4

SALAMI QUICHE
(Photograph: Unigate)

Celery and Cheese Mousse

USE THE DOUBLE-BLADED CHOPPING KNIFE.

¼ pint (⅔ cup) water
½ oz. (2½ teaspoons) gelatine
8 oz. blue cheese
4 tablespoons milk
2 tablespoons double (heavy) cream
3 celery sticks, roughly chopped
1 green pepper, seeded, roughly
  chopped and blanched
1 onion, quartered

6 stuffed olives
1 dessert apple, peeled and
  quartered
½ pint (1¼ cups) mayonnaise
2 tablespoons milk
salt and pepper
Garnish:
apple slices dipped in lemon juice
watercress sprigs

Pour the water into a small bowl and sprinkle in the gelatine. Stand the bowl in a saucepan of hot water and heat gently until the gelatine dissolves. Cool slightly. Place all the ingredients (including the dissolved gelatine) in the mixer bowl and process for a few seconds until the vegetables are roughly chopped. Taste and adjust the seasoning if necessary.

Transfer the mixture to a wetted 1½ pint (3¾ cup) mould and chill until set. Turn out onto a serving dish and decorate with the apple slices and watercress.
Serves 4

Chicken Liver Pâté

USE THE DOUBLE-BLADED CHOPPING KNIFE.

1 onion, quartered
1 clove garlic, peeled
12 oz. chicken livers
1 oz. (2 T) butter

2 tablespoons sherry
2 tablespoons tomato purée
salt and pepper
1 tablespoon double (heavy) cream

Place the onion and garlic in the mixer bowl and process until finely chopped. Remove from the bowl and set aside. Place the chicken livers, butter, sherry, tomato purée and salt and pepper in the mixer bowl and process until smooth. Add the cream and chopped onion and process for a second until well mixed.

Turn the mixture into an earthenware terrine, place in a baking tin with enough water to come halfway up the side of the terrine. Bake in a moderate oven, 325°F, Gas Mark 3 for 40 minutes or until lightly set. Leave to cool; cover and chill in the refrigerator until required.
Serves 4

MEAT

Crusty Pork Casserole

USE THE DOUBLE-BLADED CHOPPING KNIFE.

1½ lb. sparerib of pork, cut into
  pieces
1 tablespoon oil
½ lb. pork sausages
2 onions, quartered
1 clove garlic, peeled
½ oz. (2T) flour

1 pint (2½ cups) chicken stock
  (bouillon)
½ teaspoon sugar
salt and pepper
1 lb. ripe tomatoes, peeled and
  chopped
4 oz. white bread, crusts removed

Place one-third of the pork in the mixer bowl and process until roughly chopped. Repeat with remaining meat.

Heat the oil and fry the pork and sausages until brown on all sides. Cut the sausages into short lengths and place in a 3 pint (7½ cup) casserole. Put the onions and garlic in the mixer bowl and process until roughly chopped. Fry the onion mixture in the fat remaining in the pan for 5 minutes or until soft. Stir in the flour and gradually add the stock (bouillon). Bring to the boil, stirring, add the sugar, seasoning and tomatoes and pour over the meat in the casserole. Cover the casserole and cook in a moderate oven, 350°F, Gas Mark 4 for 45 minutes.

Process the bread until fine breadcrumbs are formed. Sprinkle over the top of the casserole and cook uncovered for a further 45 minutes, or until the pork is cooked through and the crumbs are crisp and golden brown.
Serves 4-6

Orange Gammon (Ham) Olives

USE THE DOUBLE–BLADED CHOPPING KNIFE.

3 oz. white bread, crusts removed
grated rind of 2 oranges
2 oz. (⅓ cup) sultanas (white
  raisins)
½ teaspoon dried thyme
½ teaspoon dried oregano
2 oz. (¼ cup) butter, melted
salt and pepper

4 thin slices gammon (ham)
juice of 2 oranges
¼ pint (⅔ cup) stock (bouillon)
1 tablespoon demerara (raw) sugar
2 teaspoons cornflour (cornstarch)
Garnish:
orange twists
watercress sprigs

In the mixer bowl place the bread, orange rind, sultanas (raisins), thyme, oregano, melted butter and seasoning. Process until the stuffing forms a ball round the knife.

Divide the stuffing between the gammon (ham) slices and roll up. Secure with wooden cocktail sticks. Arrange the olives in a shallow ovenproof dish and pour over the orange juice. Bake in a moderate oven, 350°F, Gas Mark 4 for 35–40 minutes or until the meat is cooked.

Strain the liquid into a small pan. Sprinkle the gammon (ham) with sugar and return to the oven for a further 5 minutes. Blend the cornflour (cornstarch) with a little water and stir into the liquid in the pan. Bring the liquid to the boil, stirring continuously, and cook for 1 minute. Pour the sauce over the gammon (ham) olives and garnish the dish with orange twists and watercress sprigs.
Serves 4

Farmhouse Rabbit Pie

USE THE DOUBLE-BLADED CHOPPING KNIFE.

8 oz. shortcrust pastry (basic pie
  dough), see page 68
Stuffing:
2 oz. (¼ cup) butter, melted
2 oz. streaky bacon
1 onion, quartered
2 sticks celery
3 sprigs parsley
4 slices white bread
salt and pepper

Filling:
1 oz. (2 T) lard
1 ½ lb. rabbit joints
1 onion, quartered
1 oz. (¼ cup) flour
1 pint (2 ½ cups) stock (bouillon)
2 carrots, sliced
grated rind of ½ lemon
salt and pepper

To make the stuffing, place the melted butter, bacon, onion, celery,
parsley, bread and seasoning in the mixer bowl. Process until the
stuffing forms a ball round the knife. Remove and shape into 10-12
balls.

To make the filling, melt the lard in a large frying pan (skillet), add
the rabbit joints and fry on all sides until brown. Meanwhile, process
the onion until coarsely chopped. Remove the rabbit joints from the
pan and place in a large pie dish. Fry the onion for 3 minutes or until
soft. Stir in the flour, cook for 1 minute, and gradually stir in the
stock (bouillon). Add the carrots, lemon rind and seasoning and
bring to the boil. Simmer for 5 minutes. Place the stuffing balls in
the dish and pour over the sauce.

Roll out the dough and cover the pie filling. Seal, flake and flute
the dough edges. Make leaves with pastry trimmings. Bake in a
moderately hot oven, 400°F, Gas Mark 6 for 1 hour or until the
rabbit is cooked and the pastry deep golden brown.
Serves 4-6

Cottage Pie

USE THE DOUBLE-BLADED CHOPPING KNIFE.

1 1/2 lb. potatoes, cooked and
  roughly chopped
2 tablespoons milk
1 oz. (2 T) butter
salt and pepper
1 onion, quartered
2 carrots, roughly chopped
1 lb. lean lamb, cut into 1 inch
  pieces

1 oz. (2 T) dripping
1 1/2 tablespoons flour
2 tablespoons tomato purée
3/4 pint (1 1/2 cups) stock (bouillon)
4 oz. (3/4 cup) peas
salt and pepper

Place the potatoes, milk, butter and seasoning in the mixer bowl.
Process until just smooth and remove from the bowl.

Place the onion in the mixer bowl and process until coarsely
chopped. Remove the onion and set aside. Place the carrots in the
mixer bowl and process until coarsely chopped. Remove the carrot
and set aside. Process the meat in two operations, 8 oz. (1 cup) at a
time, until it is coarsely minced (ground).

Heat the dripping in a frying pan (skillet). Add the onion and cook
until soft but not brown. Increase the heat to high, add the meat and
cook until brown on all sides. Sprinkle over the flour, mix well and
gradually stir in the tomato purée, stock, carrots, peas and seasoning.
Bring the mixture to the boil, cover with a lid and simmer for 30
minutes. Transfer the meat mixture to a baking dish, cover with the
mashed potatoes and smooth the top. Cook in a moderately hot
oven, 375°F, Gas Mark 5 for 30 minutes or until the top is golden
brown.
Serves 4

Stuffed Beef Rollups

USE THE DOUBLE-BLADED CHOPPING KNIFE.

4 sprigs parsley
4 oz. white bread
2 oz. (⅓ cup) shredded suet
½ teaspoon dried mixed herbs
grated rind of ½ lemon
salt and pepper
1 egg
8 thin slices topside (top round)
  beef

1 oz. (¼ cup) flour
1 oz. (2T) butter
1 tablespoon oil
2 onions, sliced
¾ pint (2 cups) beef stock
  (bouillon)
watercress sprigs to garnish

Place the parsley and bread in the mixer bowl and process until the bread has been reduced to large breadcrumbs. Add the suet, herbs, lemon rind, seasoning and the egg. Process until the stuffing binds into a ball around the knife.

Flatten the meat slices until thin with a rolling pin. Spread the slices with the stuffing. Roll up the meat and secure with string. Roll in the flour.

Melt the butter with the oil in a frying pan (skillet) and fry the onion slices for 5 minutes or until soft but not browned. Transfer to a 3 pint (7½ cup) casserole. Add the beef rolls to the pan and brown on all sides. Place in the casserole.

Stir any remaining flour into the pan and gradually add the stock. Bring to the boil, stirring continuously, and pour over the beef in the casserole. Season and bake in a moderate oven, 350°F, Gas Mark 4 for 1½ hours or until the meat is tender. Remove the string from the rollups and serve the meat garnished with watercress on a bed of boiled rice.

Serves 4-6

STUFFED BEEF ROLLUPS
(Photograph: Flour Advisory Bureau)

Crusty Beef Carbonnade

USE THE DOUBLE-BLADED CHOPPING KNIFE.

1½ lb. stewing steak, cut into large
  pieces
1 oz. (¼ cup) seasoned flour
1 oz. (2T) dripping
2 large onions, quartered
1 clove garlic, peeled
6 oz. (1½ cups) button mushrooms
½ pint (1¼ cups) brown ale

1 pint (2½ cups) water
salt and pepper
⅛ teaspoon nutmeg
1 teaspoon vinegar
thick slices of French bread
French mustard
½ oz. (1T) butter

Place one-third of the meat in the mixer bowl and process until the meat is cut into chunks. Repeat with remaining meat. Toss the meat in the flour. Melt the dripping in a frying pan (skillet) and brown quickly on all sides. Transfer to a 3 pint (7½ cup) casserole.

Process the onions and garlic until roughly chopped, add the mushrooms and process for another second. Transfer the vegetables to the pan and fry for 2 minutes. Stir in any remaining flour, the ale and water, seasoning, nutmeg and vinegar and pour over the meat. Cover and bake in a moderate oven, 325°F, Gas Mark 3 for 2 hours.

Spread the bread slices with a generous amount of mustard and arrange on top of the casserole. Cut the butter into small pieces and scatter them over the bread. Cook uncovered for a further 1 hour or until the meat is tender and the bread golden brown.
Serves 4-6

Shepherd's Pie

USE THE DOUBLE-BLADED CHOPPING KNIFE.

1 lb. stewing steak, cooked
1 onion, quartered
2 tablespoons stock (bouillon)
2 oz. (¼ cup) butter

salt and pepper
1½ lb. potatoes, cooked
1 egg
2 tablespoons grated Cheddar cheese

Place half the stewing steak, onion and stock (bouillon) and 1 oz. (2T) of the butter in the mixer bowl. Process until the meat is finely chopped. Place the mixture in an ovenproof dish. Repeat with remaining meat, onion and stock. Season well.

Add the potatoes, egg and remaining butter to the mixer bowl and process until the mixture is smooth. Spoon the potato into a piping bag fitted with a fluted nozzle and pipe it decoratively on top of the meat mixture. Sprinkle with the cheese and cook in a hot oven, 425°F, Gas Mark 7 for 30 minutes or until golden brown.
Serves 4

Steak Tartare

USE THE DOUBLE-BLADED CHOPPING KNIFE.

2 sprigs parsley
1 onion, quartered
1 lb. fillet steak, cut roughly into
  1 inch cubes

salt and pepper
½ tablespoon grated horseradish
4 egg yolks
2 tablespoons capers to garnish

Place the parsley in the mixer bowl, process until finely chopped and remove. Put the onion in the mixer bowl, process until finely chopped and remove.

Put half the meat in the mixer bowl with salt and pepper and the horseradish, and process until it resembles finely minced (ground) meat. Process and season the remaining meat.

Mix the meat with the chopped parsley and onion and divide between 4 plates. Make a hollow in the centre of each mound of meat and drop an egg yolk into the hollow. Chill in the refrigerator and serve garnished with capers.
Serves 4

Stuffed Shoulder of Lamb

USE THE DOUBLE-BLADED CHOPPING KNIFE.

6 oz. streaky bacon
3 oz. white bread, crusts removed
3 tablespoons chopped fresh mint
salt and pepper

beaten egg
4-4 ½ lb. shoulder of lamb, with
 the blade bone removed

Place the bacon and bread in the mixer bowl and process until finely
chopped. Add the mint and seasoning. With the motor running, pour
enough beaten egg through the feed tube to make the stuffing form a
ball round the knife. Press the stuffing into the cavity where the bone
was removed. Tie up the meat neatly with string. Weigh the joint.
Place the meat in a roasting tin. Cook in a moderately hot oven,
375°F, Gas Mark 5 allowing 20 minutes per lb. plus 30 minutes over.
Remove the string. Serve the lamb with boiled potatoes and mixed
vegetables.
Serves 4-6

Minty Lemon Lamb

USE THE DOUBLE-BLADED CHOPPING KNIFE.

1 onion, quartered
2 oz. (¼ cup) butter, melted
4 oz. white bread, crusts removed
grated rind and juice of 1 lemon
small bunch parsley

1 teaspoon mint sauce
salt and pepper
2 ½ lb. breast of lamb
parsley sprigs to garnish

In the mixer bowl place the onion, melted butter, bread, lemon rind
and juice, parsley, mint sauce and seasoning. Process until the
stuffing forms a ball round the knife.
 Spread the breast of lamb with the stuffing and roll up. Tie
securely with string. Place meat on a rack in a roasting tin and bake
in a moderatley hot oven, 375°F, Gas Mark 5 for 30 minutes per lb.
Serve garnished with parsley sprigs.
Serves 4-6

STUFFED SHOULDER OF LAMB
(Photograph: New Zealand Lamb)

Veal Birds

USE THE DOUBLE-BLADED CHOPPING KNIFE.

6 escalopes of veal, beaten until
  thin
salt and pepper
6 slices ham
6 slices Gruyère cheese

1 egg, beaten
4 oz. (1 cup) fresh white
  breadcrumbs
3 oz. (⅓ cup) margarine
3 tablespoons oil

Lay the veal escalopes on a board and season generously. Cover half of each escalope with a slice of ham and cheese. Fold over and press edges together. Dip the meat in the egg and coat with breadcrumbs twice. Melt the margarine and oil in a large frying pan and fry the veal until golden brown, turning once. When cooked (about 10-15 minutes) the Gruyère cheese should be just melting.

    Serve the veal birds with Duchesse potatoes, broccoli, carrots and onions.

Serves 6

Chicken Croquettes

USE THE DOUBLE-BLADED CHOPPING KNIFE AND THE GRATING DISC
ATTACHMENT.

1 oz. (¼ cup) walnuts
8 oz. (1 cup) cooked chicken, cut
  into 1 inch pieces
2 shallots, halved
2 teaspoons chopped fresh tarragon
1 oz. (2 T) butter
1½ oz. (⅓ cup) flour

¼ pint (⅔ cup) milk
2 oz. Cheddar cheese
salt and pepper
1 egg, beaten
rolled oats for coating
fat for frying

Using the double-bladed chopping knife, process the walnuts until finely chopped. Remove and set aside. Place the chicken, shallots and tarragon in the mixer bowl and process until the chicken is very finely chopped. Melt the butter in a saucepan, add the chicken mixture and the nuts and cook for 5 minutes. Mix in the flour and gradually blend in the milk, stirring continuously. Bring to the boil and cook for 2 minutes. Process the cheese through the grating disc attachment. Add to the sauce and season well. Cool the mixture, then chill in the refrigerator.

    Divide the mixture into 8 and roll into croquette shapes on a well-floured board. Dip into beaten egg, drain and coat with rolled oats. Deep fry in hot fat until golden brown.

Serves 3-4

FISH

Fish Curry

USE THE DOUBLE–BLADED CHOPPING KNIFE.

1 large onion, quartered
2 carrots, roughly chopped
1 green pepper, seeded
1 cooking apple, peeled and cored
1½ oz. (3T) margarine
4 teaspoons curry powder

1 tablespoon flour
1 tablespoon vinegar
½ pint (1¼ cups) chicken stock
 (bouillon)
1 lb. white fish, skinned and cut
 into pieces

Place the onion and carrots in the mixer bowl, process until roughly chopped and remove. Add the green pepper and cooking apple to the mixer bowl, and process until roughly chopped and remove.

Melt the margarine in a large saucepan and fry the onion and carrots for 3 minutes or until the onion is soft. Stir in the pepper and apple, curry powder, flour, vinegar and stock. Bring to the boil, stirring continuously, and cook for 3 minutes.

Place half the fish in the mixer bowl and process until roughly chopped. Repeat with remaining fish. Add the fish to the sauce and simmer, covered, for 15-25 minutes or until the fish is tender. Serve with rice.

Serves 4

Tuna Paste

USE THE DOUBLE-BLADED CHOPPING KNIFE.

1 × 3½ oz. can tuna fish, drained
4 oz. (½ cup) butter, roughly
  chopped
salt and pepper

dash of Tabasco sauce
lemon juice to taste
1 tablespoon chopped fresh parsley

Place all the ingredients in the mixer bowl and process until the tuna fish and butter are well mixed. Chill in the refrigerator.
  Serve with melba toast.

Sardine Flan

USE THE DOUBLE-BLADED CHOPPING KNIFE.

8 oz. shortcrust pastry (basic pie
  dough), see page 68
Filling:
¼ pint (⅔ cup) milk
2 eggs

salt and pepper
6 tomatoes, peeled
½ teaspoon dried mixed herbs
1 large onion, quartered
2 × 4⅜ oz. cans sardines, drained

Roll out the dough and line a 7 inch flan ring.
  Place the milk, eggs, seasoning, 4 of the tomatoes, the herbs, onion and half of the sardines in the mixer bowl. Process until fairly smooth and pour into the flan case. Slice the remaining tomatoes and arrange round the edge of the flan and place the sardines in a wheel shape in the middle.
  Bake in a moderately hot oven, 375°F, Gas Mark 5 for 40 minutes or until the pastry is golden brown and the filling set.
  Serve hot or cold.
Serves 6

SARDINE FLAN
(Photograph: Stork Margarine)

Smoked Mackerel Mousse

USE THE DOUBLE-BLADED CHOPPING KNIFE.

12 oz. smoked mackerel fillets, cut
  into pieces
1 pint (2½ cups) mayonnaise
¼ pint (⅔ cup) double (heavy)
  cream
½ oz. (2½ teaspoons) gelatine
  dissolved in 3 tablespoons hot
  water

a few drops Worcestershire sauce
1 teaspoon lemon juice
salt and pepper
3 egg whites
cucumber slices to garnish

Place the mackerel in the mixer bowl. Add the mayonnaise, cream, dissolved gelatine, Worcestershire sauce, lemon, salt and pepper. Process until fairly smooth.

Whisk the egg whites until stiff. Spoon into the mixer bowl and process for a second. Pour the mixture into a wetted 1½ pint (3¾ cup) mould. Chill until set. Release the mixture from the side of the mould and turn out onto a serving dish. Decorate the mousse with cucumber slices.

Serves 4-6

Mackerel and Tomato Loaf

USE THE DOUBLE-BLADED CHOPPING KNIFE.

1 large onion, quartered
1 oz. (2 T) butter
2 × 15 oz. cans mackerel steaks in
  tomato
3 large tomatoes, halved
8 oz. white bread slices, crusts
  removed
salt and cayenne pepper

3 teaspoons lemon juice
2 tablespoons chopped fresh parsley
¼ pint (⅔ cup) milk
1 egg, beaten
Garnish:
mashed potato
stuffed olives

Place the onion in the mixer bowl. Process until roughly chopped. Melt the butter and gently fry the onion until soft but not browned. Put the onion and butter in the mixer bowl and add the mackerel, tomatoes, bread, seasoning to taste, lemon juice, parsley, milk and egg and process until fairly smooth.

Place in a well-greased loaf tin and cook in a moderately hot oven, 375°F, Gas Mark 5 for 1-1½ hours or until it has shrunk slightly from the sides of the tin and is golden brown. When cooked turn out onto a serving dish and decorate with piped mashed potato and sliced stuffed olives.

This dish may be served hot or cold.

Serves 8

Tuna Bake with Cheese Swirls

USE THE DOUBLE-BLADED CHOPPING KNIFE.

Cheese Swirls
8 oz. (2 cups) plain (all-purpose)
  flour
3 teaspoons baking powder
½ teaspoon salt
2 oz. (¼ cup) butter
3 fl. oz. (⅜ cup) milk
4 oz. cheese
Sauce:
1 medium onion, quartered
1 large green pepper, seeded

1 oz. (2 T) butter
2 tablespoons flour
1 × 10½ oz. can condensed
  chicken soup
1 pint (2½ cups) milk
salt and pepper
2 tablespoons lemon juice
2 × 7 oz. cans tuna fish

Place the flour, baking powder and salt in the mixer bowl with the butter. Process until the mixture resembles fine breadcrumbs. With the motor running add just enough milk through the feed tube to make the dough form a ball round the knife. Place the dough in a polythene (plastic) bag and chill in the refrigerator for 30 minutes.

Process the cheese in the mixer bowl until finely chopped.

Roll out the dough to a rectangle ¼ inch thick. Sprinkle half of the cheese over the dough. Roll up the dough like a Swiss (jelly) roll, and cut into ½ inch thick slices. Lay slices on a baking sheet and bake in a hot oven, 425°F, Gas Mark 7 for 15 minutes or until just cooked.

Place the onion in the mixer bowl and process until roughly chopped. Remove. Add the green pepper and process for a second.

Melt the butter and fry the onion and green pepper for 5 minutes. Stir in the flour and cook for 1 minute. Gradually add the soup, milk, seasoning and lemon juice, stirring continuously. Bring the sauce to the boil, stirring all the time. Add the tuna and pour the sauce into a casserole. Top the sauce with the cheese swirls and bake in a moderately hot oven, 375°F, Gas Mark 5 for 15-20 minutes or until the swirls are golden brown.
Serves 4

Tuna Loaf

USE THE DOUBLE-BLADED CHOPPING KNIFE.

1 lb. haddock fillet
3 oz. white bread slices, crusts
  removed
2 × 7 oz. cans tuna fish
3 oz. brown bread slices, crusts
  removed
½ teaspoon paprika
1 medium onion, quartered

1 oz. (2 T) butter
salt and pepper
1 egg, beaten
Garnish:
parsley sprigs
cucumber slices
pimiento
lemon wedges

Put half the haddock and half the white bread in the mixer bowl and process until finely chopped. Repeat with the remaining haddock and white bread. Remove and reserve.

Process the tuna, brown bread and paprika. Remove and reserve.

Place the onion in the mixer bowl and process until finely chopped. Melt the butter in a saucepan and cook the onion until soft. Add half of the onion to the haddock mixture and half to the tuna mixture. Season both mixtures and bind each with a little of the beaten egg.

Divide the haddock mixture into 4 and the tuna mixture into 5 pieces and place alternate pieces, vertically, in a well-greased loaf tin.

Bake in a moderate oven, 350°F, Gas Mark 4 for 1 hour or until the mixture has shrunk away slightly from the sides. Cool in the tin.

Garnish the loaf with parsley, cucumber, pimiento and lemon wedges.
Serves 6

TUNA LOAF
(Photograph: John West Foods)

Salmon Balls with Piquant Sauce

USE THE DOUBLE-BLADED CHOPPING KNIFE.

4 slices white bread, crusts removed
1 × 7½ oz. can pink salmon,
  drained
2¼ oz. instant potato granules,
  made up as instructed
1 tablespoon tomato ketchup
cayenne pepper
1 oz. (¼ cup) plain flour
2 eggs, beaten
fat for deep frying

Sauce:
2 tablespoons mayonnaise
1 tablespoon tomato chutney
½ tablespoon chopped fresh chives
1 cap pimiento
½ small green pepper, seeded
½ teaspoon paprika

Cut the bread into fingers, place in the mixer bowl and process to very fine crumbs. Remove and reserve.

Place the salmon in the mixer bowl, add the potato, tomato ketchup and cayenne pepper to taste. Process until fairly smooth. Divide the mixture into bite-sized pieces and roll into balls. Roll in the flour and then coat completely with egg and cover with the breadcrumbs. Fry the balls in hot fat until golden brown. Drain thoroughly.

In the mixer bowl place the mayonnaise, chutney, chives, pimiento, green pepper and paprika. Process to mix. Serve the sauce in a small bowl with the salmon balls, plus a supply of cocktail sticks.

Serves 6

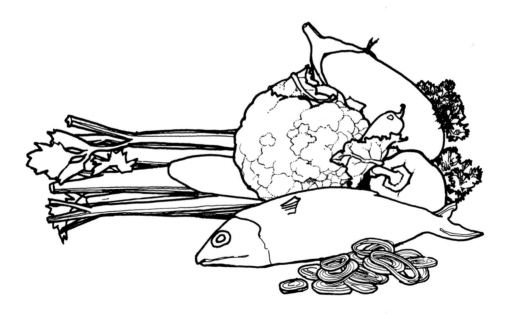

Scalloped Salmon

USE THE DOUBLE-BLADED CHOPPING KNIFE.

4 slices white bread, crusts removed
1 × 7½ oz. can pink salmon,
  drained and juices reserved
1½ oz. (3 T) butter
1½ oz. (⅜ cup) flour

¾ pint (2 cups) milk and salmon
  liquid
3 oz. cheese
salt and pepper

Butter 4 scallop shells or 4 individual ovenproof dishes. Place the bread in the mixer bowl and process to fine crumbs. Coat the insides of the shells or dishes with some of the breadcrumbs. Flake the salmon and pile some into each shell or dish.

Melt the butter in a saucepan, stir in the flour and cook for 1 minute, gradually add the milk and salmon liquid, stirring continuously. Bring to the boil, still stirring, and cook for 1 minute.

Process the cheese until chopped and add two-thirds of it to the sauce. Season the sauce. Pour the sauce over the salmon. Sprinkle with the remaining breadcrumbs and cheese and brown under the grill (broiler) until crisp and golden brown.

Serves 4

Savoury Soufflé Omelette

USE THE DOUBLE-BLADED CHOPPING KNIFE.

4 eggs, separated
2 tablespoons cold water
½ teaspoon salt
pepper

Filling:
7 oz. kipper fillets
4 spring onions (scallions)
1 tomato, quartered
rind and juice of ½ lemon
lemon wedges to garnish

Place the egg yolks in the mixer bowl, add the water and seasoning. Process for a second to mix. Whisk the egg whites until stiff. Add the whisked egg whites to the mixer bowl and process for one second, enough to just mix the ingredients.

Pour the omelette mixture into a lightly oiled frying pan (skillet) and cook gently for 1½ minutes. Lift the pan off the heat and put it under a hot grill (broiler) until the omelette is well risen and golden brown.

Meanwhile, place the kipper fillets, spring onions (scallions), tomato, lemon rind and juice and pepper in the mixer bowl and process until roughly chopped. Spoon the filling onto one half of the omelette and fold over. Serve the omelette on a hot plate with lemon wedges.

Serves 2

Kipper Cakes

USE THE DOUBLE-BLADED CHOPPING KNIFE.

6 slices white bread, crusts removed
  and cut into fingers
1 lb. potatoes, cooked
1 × 15 oz. can kipper fillets,
  drained
2 eggs, hard-boiled and halved
2 tablespoons chopped fresh parsley
salt and pepper

dash Tabasco sauce
1 teaspoon lemon juice
2 eggs, beaten
2 tablespoons flour
fat for deep frying
Garnish:
lemon slices
parsley sprigs

Place the bread in the mixer bowl and process to fine crumbs. Remove and reserve.

   Place the potatoes and kipper fillets in the mixer bowl and process until very smooth. Add the hard-boiled eggs, parsley, seasoning, Tabasco sauce and lemon juice. Process for a second and then add just enough beaten egg through the feed tube to bind to a stiff mixture.

   Form the mixture into croquette shapes. Coat the croquettes in the flour, then in the remaining beaten egg and finally in the breadcrumbs. Fry the croquettes until golden brown and crisp. Drain on kitchen paper and serve the croquettes very hot, garnished with lemon slices and parsley sprigs.
Serves 3-4

Egg and Shrimp Cocktail

USE THE DOUBLE-BLADED CHOPPING KNIFE.

¼ pint (⅔ cup) mayonnaise
¼ pint (⅔ cup) red wine
5 oz. carton (⅔ cup) soured cream

4 oz. (½ cup) shrimps
4 eggs, hard-boiled and halved
salt and pepper

Place the mayonnaise, red wine, soured cream, shrimps, eggs and seasoning in the mixer bowl and process until roughly blended (don't process to a purée). Chill and serve in glasses with vegetable sticks or salad.
Serves 4

KIPPER CAKES
(Photograph: John West Foods)

VEGETABLES AND SALADS

Ratatouille

USE THE SLICING DISC ATTACHMENT.

3 medium aubergines (eggplant),
  quartered
salt and pepper
2 large onions, quartered
1 clove garlic, peeled

1 green pepper, seeded
3 small courgettes (zucchini)
4 oz. (½ cup) margarine
4 large tomatoes, peeled
bouquet garni

Process the aubergines (eggplant) through the slicing disc
attachment. Cover generously with salt and leave for 30 minutes.
Drain, then rinse thoroughly and pat dry with kitchen paper. Process
the onions, garlic, pepper and courgettes (zucchini) through the
slicing disc attachment.

   Melt the margarine in a large saucepan. Add the onions, garlic and
pepper, cover the pan and cook for 5 minutes or until soft but not
browned. Add the aubergines (eggplant), courgettes (zucchini),
tomatoes, seasoning and bouquet garni to the pan. Cover and cook
gently for 30 minutes or until the vegetables are tender. Remove the
bouquet garni.

   Serve hot or cold.
Serves 4-6

Potato Croquettes

USE THE DOUBLE-BLADED CHOPPING KNIFE.

4 slices stale bread, crusts removed
2 slices bacon, grilled (broiled) and
  roughly chopped
1 lb. cooked potatoes, quartered

½ oz. (1 T) butter, melted
2 eggs
salt and pepper
oil for deep frying

Place the bread in the mixer bowl and process to fine breadcrumbs. Remove and reserve.

Place the bacon in the mixer bowl and process for a second. Add the potatoes with the butter, 1 egg and seasoning and process for 5 seconds.

Chill the mixture in the refrigerator until firm. Shape the mixture into a long roll on a floured surface. Cut into 8 croquettes and coat with the remaining beaten egg and then the breadcrumbs.

Fry the croquettes in hot oil until golden brown. Drain on kitchen paper. Serve immediately.
Serves 3-4

Potato Cake

USE THE DOUBLE-BLADED CHOPPING KNIFE.

1 lb. cooked potatoes, quartered
2 oz. (¼ cup) butter
4 oz. (1 cup) plain (all-purpose)
  flour

salt and pepper
4 tablespoons milk
1 tablespoon chopped fresh chives
oil for frying

Place the potatoes in the mixer bowl with all the remaining ingredients, except the oil. Process for just long enough to mash the potatoes.

On a floured surface roll out the potato mixture to a round.

Fry the potato cake in hot oil, turning once, until golden brown on both sides. Drain the potato cake on kitchen paper and serve immediately.
Serves 4-6

Potato and Onion Layer

USE THE SLICING DISC ATTACHMENT AND THE GRATING DISC
ATTACHMENT.

1 1/2 lb. potatoes, halved or
  quartered
3 onions, quartered
2 oz. cheese

salt and pepper
1/4 pint (2/3 cup) milk
2 oz. (1/4 cup) margarine
tomato wedges to garnish

Process the potatoes and onions, separately, through the slicing disc
attachment. Remove. Fit the grating disc attachment and process the
cheese.

Layer the potato and onion slices in a casserole, sprinkling each
layer with a little salt and pepper and ending with a layer of potato
slices.

Pour the milk into the casserole and dot the potato with the
margarine. Cover the casserole with foil and bake in a moderate
oven, 350°F, Gas Mark 4 for 50 minutes or until the potatoes are
cooked. Remove the foil and sprinkle over the grated cheese and
cook for a further 10 minutes to melt the cheese and brown the top.
Garnish with the tomato wedges and serve immediately.
Serves 4-6

Creamed Spinach

USE THE DOUBLE-BLADED CHOPPING KNIFE.

2 lb. fresh spinach
salt and pepper
a few slices of leek
1 oz. (2 T) butter

1-2 tablespoons double (heavy)
  cream
1/2 teaspoon celery seeds

Cook the spinach in a little boiling, salted water until tender. Drain
well. Place the spinach and leek in the mixer bowl and process until
the spinach is finely chopped.

Melt the butter in a saucepan, add the spinach and heat through.
Stir in the cream and seasonings.
Serves 3-4

POTATO AND ONION LAYER
(Photograph: Stork Margarine)

Oriental Vegetable Casserole

USE THE SLICING DISC ATTACHMENT AND THE DOUBLE-BLADED CHOPPING KNIFE.

1 lb. courgettes (zucchini)
1 lb. carrots
1 small piece of fresh ginger, peeled
1 clove garlic, peeled
1 oz. (2T) margarine
1 teaspoon sugar

4 tablespoons water
4 tablespoons wine vinegar
salt and pepper
¼ teaspoon paprika pepper
½ teaspoon cumin seeds

Using the slicing disc attachment process the courgettes (zucchini) and carrots. Remove. Fit the double-bladed chopping knife in the mixer bowl and process the ginger and garlic until roughly chopped.

Melt the margarine in a large saucepan, add the chopped garlic and ginger and the sugar and cook for 2 minutes. Add the sliced courgettes (zucchini) and carrots, the water, vinegar, salt, peppers and cumin. Bring to the boil and simmer gently for 10-20 minutes depending on how crisp you like your vegetables.
Serves 4

Lentil Purée

USE THE DOUBLE-BLADED CHOPPING KNIFE.

1 lb. (2 cups) lentils
1 onion, roughly chopped
1 carrot, roughly chopped
salt and pepper

2 bay leaves
2 oz. (¼ cup) butter
¼ pint (⅔ cup) single (thin) cream

Cover the lentils with cold water and leave them to soak overnight.

Place the soaked lentils with the soaking liquid in a large saucepan with the onion, carrot, a little salt and the bay leaves. Add enough water to just cover the ingredients in the pan. Bring the liquid to the boil, cover and simmer for 1½ hours or until the lentils are soft. Drain well and remove the bay leaves.

Put the lentil mixture in the mixer bowl and process to a purée. Spoon the purée into a saucepan, reheat over low heat, then beat in the butter and cream. Taste and adjust the seasoning if necessary.
Serves 4-6

Mixed Salad Platter

USE THE GRATING DISC ATTACHMENT, THE SLICING DISC ATTACHMENT
AND THE DOUBLE-BLADED CHOPPING KNIFE.

2 large carrots, cut into 1 inch
  pieces
2 oz. Cheddar cheese
1 small onion, halved
1/4 cucumber
2 sticks celery

1 red pepper, seeded and quartered
1 large eating apple, cored and
  quartered
1/4 white cabbage, roughly chopped
sprigs of watercress to garnish
mayonnaise for serving

Fit the grating disc attachment and process, separately, the carrots,
cheese and onion. Remove and set aside.

Fit the slicing disc attachment and process, separately, the
cucumber, celery and pepper. Remove and set aside.

Fit the double-bladed chopping knife and process, separately, the
apple and cabbage.

Toss all the ingredients together and arrange in a salad bowl.
Garnish with watercress and serve with mayonnaise.
Serves 4

Raw Carrot Salad

USE THE GRATING DISC ATTACHMENT AND THE DOUBLE-BLADED
CHOPPING KNIFE.

1 lb. young carrots
2 tablespoons olive oil
2 teaspoons white wine vinegar

3 tablespoons soured cream
salt and pepper

Process the carrots through the grating disc attachment. Place in a
bowl.

Fit the double-bladed chopping knife in the mixer bowl and add
the olive oil, vinegar, soured cream and seasoning. Process until the
ingredients are well mixed.

Pour the dressing over the carrots and chill before serving.
Serves 4

Coleslaw

USE THE GRATING DISC ATTACHMENT.

½ white cabbage
1 medium carrot
1 stick celery
1 medium onion
1 red apple, cored

¼ green pepper, seeded
2 tablespoons raisins
1 oz. walnuts
¼ pint (⅔ cup) mayonnaise

Cut the vegetables into rough chunks. Fit the grating disc attachment and process the cabbage, carrot, celery, onion, apple and pepper.

Place the grated vegetables in a large bowl. Add the raisins, walnuts and mayonnaise and mix thoroughly to coat the vegetables with the mayonnaise.

Serves 4

Mayonnaise

USE THE DOUBLE-BLADED CHOPPING KNIFE.

2 egg yolks
½ teaspoon English mustard
½ pint (1¼ cups) olive oil
1 tablespoon lemon juice

½ teaspoon salt
¼ teaspoon black pepper
½ teaspoon sugar

Place the yolks in the mixer bowl with the mustard and a spoonful of the oil. Process to blend. With the motor running pour the oil, a few drops at a time, through the feed tube. The mixture should be thick and creamy. When all the oil has been absorbed, leave the motor running and gradually pour in the lemon juice. Then add the salt, pepper and sugar. Chill in the refrigerator until required.

French Dressing

USE THE DOUBLE-BLADED CHOPPING KNIFE.

4 tablespoons olive oil
1 teaspoon French mustard
¼ teaspoon sugar

1 tablespoon white wine vinegar
salt and pepper
¼ teaspoon dried mixed herbs

Place the oil, mustard, sugar, vinegar, seasoning and herbs in the mixer bowl and process until blended. Serve chilled.

The dressing may be stored in the refrigerator. Re-blend before using if necessary.

SAVOURY PANCAKES *(page 28)*
(Photograph: British Egg Information Service)

CAKES, PASTRY AND BREAD

Victoria Sandwich

USE THE DOUBLE-BLADED CHOPPING KNIFE.

4 oz. (½ cup) butter
4 oz. (½ cup) castor sugar
2 eggs
4 oz. (1 cup) self-raising flour,
  sifted

grated rind of 1 small lemon
4 tablespoons raspberry jam
extra castor (superfine) sugar for
  dusting

Grease and flour two 6 inch sandwich tins (layer cake pans).
   Place the butter and sugar in the mixer bowl and process until
light and fluffy. With the machine running, add the eggs, one at a
time, processing after each addition until the mixture is smooth.
Switch off the motor, add the sifted flour and lemon rind and process
for a second to mix.
   Divide the mixture between the two sandwich tins (layer cake
pans).
   Bake in a moderate oven, 350°F, Gas Mark 4 for 25–30 minutes or
until light golden brown. Turn out the cakes on to a wire rack to
cool. Spread jam over one cake layer, then sandwich the two cakes
together. Sprinkle the top with castor (superfine) sugar.
Makes one 6 inch round cake

Chocolate Cake

USE THE DOUBLE-BLADED CHOPPING KNIFE.

5 oz. (1¼ cups) self-raising flour
1 oz. (¼ cup) vanilla-flavoured
  custard powder
1 oz. (¼ cup) cocoa powder
  (unsweetened)

6 oz. (¾ cup) butter
6 oz. (¾ cup) sugar
3 eggs
2 tablespoons milk
whipped cream for filling

Grease and line two 8 inch sandwich tins (layer cake pans).
  Sift the flour, custard powder and cocoa together twice.
  Place the butter and sugar in the mixer bowl and process until light and fluffy. With the motor running add one egg and one-third of the flour mixture and process. Repeat this processing twice. Add the milk and process to mix.
  Divide the mixture between the prepared tins and bake in a moderate oven, 350°F, Gas Mark 4 for 30–35 minutes or until well risen and firm. Remove from the tins and cool on a wire rack. When cold, sandwich together with whipped cream.
Makes one 8 inch round cake

Gingerbread

USE THE DOUBLE-BLADED CHOPPING KNIFE.

4 oz. (½ cup) butter
2 oz. (⅓ cup) soft (light) brown
  sugar
6 oz. (½ cup) black treacle
  (molasses)
3 tablespoons golden (light corn)
  syrup
¼ pint (⅔ cup) milk

2 eggs
8 oz. (2 cups) plain (all-purpose)
  flour
1 teaspoon mixed spice
2 teaspoons ground ginger
1 teaspoon bicarbonate of soda
  (baking soda)

Grease and line a 2 lb. loaf tin. In a saucepan heat together the butter, sugar, treacle (molasses) and syrup until they have melted. Remove from the heat and cool.
  Pour the butter mixture into the mixer bowl, add the milk, eggs, flour, spices and soda. Process until the mixture is smooth, scraping down the flour from the sides of the bowl with a plastic spatula halfway through, if necessary.
  Pour the mixture into the prepared tin. Bake in a cool oven, 300°F, Gas Mark 2 for 1¼–1½ hours or until a skewer inserted in the centre comes out clean.
  Cool slightly in the tin. Cool on a wire rack and serve cut in slices.
Makes one 2 lb. loaf

Marshmallow Cake

USE THE DOUBLE-BLADED CHOPPING KNIFE.

6 oz. (¾ cup) margarine
6 oz. (¾ cup) castor sugar
2 eggs
7½ oz. (1¾ cups) plain
  (all-purpose) flour, sieved
⅛ teaspoon salt

3 teaspoons baking powder
6 tablespoons milk
Filling and Topping:
apricot jam
16 marshmallows
1 oz. (¼ cup) chopped walnuts

Place the butter and sugar in the mixer bowl and process until light and fluffy. With the machine running add the eggs one at a time, processing until the mixture is smooth after each addition.

Switch off the machine, add the sieved flour, salt, baking powder and milk. Process for a second. Divide between two 8 inch sandwich tins (layer cake pans). Bake in a moderately hot oven, 375°F, Gas Mark 5 for 30 minutes or until golden brown.

Cool the cakes on a wire rack. Spread the top and sides of both cakes with apricot jam. Place 9 marshmallows on the jam side of one cake, not too close to the edge, and put into a hot oven, 425°F, Gas Mark 7 for a few minutes until the marshmallows start to melt. Repeat with 7 marshmallows on the top of the second cake. Sandwich the cakes together, marshmallow sides uppermost, and sprinkle the top with walnuts.

Leave to cool before cutting.
Makes one 8 inch round cake

MARSHMALLOW CAKE, GINGERBREAD *(page 63)*, MAIDS OF HONOUR *(page 66)*, BUTTERFLY CAKES *(page 67)*, ORANGE AND GRAPEFRUIT CHEESECAKE *(page 70)*
(Photograph: Unigate)

Maids of Honour

USE THE DOUBLE-BLADED CHOPPING KNIFE.

6 oz. shortcrust pastry (basic pie
  dough), see page 68
2-3 tablespoons raspberry jam
2 oz. (¼ cup) butter
2 oz. (¼ cup) castor sugar
1 egg

2 oz. (½ cup) cake crumbs
2 oz. (½ cup) ground almonds
1 tablespoon milk
Decoration:
white glacé icing
glacé cherries

Roll out the pastry and line 12 tartlet tins (patty shells). Spread a little jam in the base of each.

In the mixer bowl process the butter and sugar until light and fluffy. With the motor running add the egg. Switch off the motor and add the cake crumbs, ground almonds and milk. Process until mixed.

Put spoonfuls of the mixture into each pastry case. Bake in a moderately hot oven, 375°F, Gas Mark 5 for 20–30 minutes or until the pastry is light brown and the filling set.

Cool on a wire rack. Decorate each cake with a little glacé icing and a cherry.

Makes 12 pastries

Shortbread

USE THE DOUBLE-BLADED CHOPPING KNIFE.

6 oz. (1½ cups) plain
  (all-purpose) flour, sifted
2 oz. (¼ cup) castor sugar

grated rind of 1 small lemon
4 oz. (½ cup) butter

Place the flour, sugar, lemon rind and butter in the mixer bowl and process until the mixture forms a ball round the knife.

Press the dough into a round about ½ inch thick on a baking sheet. Mark the round into 8 sections and pinch the edges decoratively. Prick all over with a fork.

Bake in a cool oven, 300°F, Gas Mark 2 for 1 hour or until just turning light golden brown at the edges. Transfer to a wire rack to cool.

Makes 8 biscuits (cookies)

Butterfly Cakes

USE THE DOUBLE-BLADED CHOPPING KNIFE.

4 oz. (½ cup) butter
4 oz. (½ cup) castor sugar
2 eggs
4 oz. (1 cup) self-raising flour

Filling:
4 oz. (½ cup) butter
8 oz. (1¾ cups) icing
 (confectioners') sugar, sifted
1 tablespoon milk
icing (confectioners') sugar for
 dusting

Place the butter and sugar in the mixer bowl and process until light and fluffy. With the motor running, add an egg and process until the mixture is smooth. Repeat with the other egg. Switch off the machine, add the flour and process for a second.

Spoon the mixture into 16–18 paper cases and bake in a moderately hot oven, 375°F, Gas Mark 5 for 20–25 minutes or until golden brown. Cool on a wire rack.

In the mixer bowl place the butter, sugar and milk. Process until light and fluffy.

Slice the tops off the cakes and cut each top in half. Pipe a swirl of the butter icing on top of each cake and press in the halved tops to form wings. Dust lightly with icing (confectioners') sugar.

Makes about 16 cakes

Shortcrust Pastry (Basic Pie Dough)

USE THE DOUBLE-BLADED CHOPPING KNIFE.

8 oz. (2 cups) plain (all-purpose) flour
½ teaspoon salt

2 oz. (¼ cup) margarine
2 oz. (¼ cup) lard (shortening)
a little cold water

Place the flour, salt, margarine and lard (shortening) in the mixer bowl and process until the mixture resembles fine breadcrumbs. With the motor running add just enough water through the feed tube to make the dough form a ball round the knife.

Place the dough in a polythene (plastic) bag and chill in a refrigerator for 30 minutes before rolling out.

Makes 8 oz. shortcrust pastry (basic pie dough)

Orange and Apple Flan

USE THE DOUBLE-BLADED CHOPPING KNIFE AND THE SLICING DISC ATTACHMENT.

8 oz. shortcrust pastry (basic pie dough), see above
1 lb. cooking apples
2 tablespoons water

2 tablespoons sugar
2 dessert apples
1 orange, cut into segments
1 cherry

Roll out the pastry and line a 7 inch fluted flan ring. Bake 'blind' in a moderately hot oven, 400°F, Gas Mark 6 for 15–20 minutes until just cooked.

Peel and core the cooking apples. Place in a saucepan with the water and sugar and cook for 15–20 minutes or until very soft. Place the apples in the mixer bowl fitted with the double-bladed chopping knife and process until smooth. Pour into the flan case.

Core the dessert apples. Fit the slicing disc attachment and process the apples. Arrange the apple slices in a wheel shape on top of the apple purée. Return to the oven for 10 minutes to warm through. Decorate with the orange segments and cherry.

Serve hot or cold.

Serves 4-6

ORANGE AND APPLE FLAN
(Photograph: Stork Margarine)

Orange and Grapefruit Cheesecake

USE THE DOUBLE-BLADED CHOPPING KNIFE.

8 oz. digestive biscuits (Graham crackers)
3 oz. (³/4 cup) icing (confectioners') sugar
4 oz. (¹/2 cup) butter

Filling:
1 packet orange jelly (orange flavored gelatin)
2 tablespoons water
1 egg, separated
¹/4 pint (²/3 cup) milk
grated rind and juice of 1 small grapefruit
1 oz. (2 T) castor sugar
4 oz. (¹/2 cup) cottage cheese
grated orange rind to decorate

Place the biscuits (Graham crackers) and icing (confectioners') sugar in the mixer bowl and process until the biscuits are fine crumbs. Melt the butter in a saucepan, add the biscuit crumbs and mix thoroughly. Cover the base of a loose-bottomed cake tin and pack the crumbs firmly.

Dissolve the jelly (gelatin) in the water. Add the egg yolk and milk, stir over the heat for a few minutes, but do not boil. Pour the mixture into the mixer bowl. Add the grapefruit rind and juice, sugar and cottage cheese and process until smooth.

Whisk the egg white until stiff and add to the mixer bowl. Process for a second. Pour the mixture into the cake tin and leave in a cool place to set. Lift the cheesecake out of the tin with the loose base. Transfer to a serving plate and decorate with orange rind.

Serves 6

Lemon Cheesecake

USE THE DOUBLE-BLADED CHOPPING KNIFE.

8 oz. digestive biscuits (Graham crackers)
4 oz. (¹/2 cup) butter
8 oz. (1 cup) cream cheese
3 eggs
juice of 1 lemon
4 oz. (¹/2 cup) castor sugar

Break up the biscuits (crackers) and place in the mixer bowl. Add the butter and process until well mixed. Press into an 8 inch flan tin (pie pan).

Place the cheese, eggs, lemon juice and sugar in the mixer bowl and process until smooth. Pour into the flan case. Bake in a moderate oven, 350°F, Gas Mark 4 for 30 minutes or until lightly set.

Serves 4-6

Baps

USE THE DOUBLE-BLADED CHOPPING KNIFE.

1 lb. (4 cups) strong (bread) flour
2 oz. (¼ cup) lard (shortening)
½ teaspoon sugar
½ oz. fresh (½ cake compressed)
  yeast

½ pint (1 ¼ cups) warm milk
1 teaspoon salt
flour for dusting

Place the flour, lard (shortening) and sugar in the mixer bowl and process until the mixture resembles fine breadcrumbs. Mix the yeast with half the milk and leave until frothy. Dissolve the salt in the remaining milk.

With the motor running pour in the yeast liquid and remaining milk through the feed tube and process until the dough is well mixed. Process a further 60 seconds to knead.

Remove the dough to an oiled bowl, cover with a damp cloth and leave in a warm place for 1 hour or until it has doubled in size.

Turn the dough onto a well-floured surface, knead lightly and divide into 8 rounds. Place on a floured baking sheet. Flatten the baps and cover with an oiled polythene (plastic) bag. Leave for about 20 minutes or until almost doubled in size. Remove from the bag.

Dust with flour and bake in a hot oven, 450°F, Gas Mark 8 for 20-25 minutes or until they are lightly browned and sound hollow when tapped underneath. Transfer to a wire rack to cool.
Makes 8

Basic White Bread

USE THE DOUBLE-BLADED CHOPPING KNIFE.

¼ oz. fresh (¼ cake compressed)
  yeast
¼ pint (⅔ cup) warm water
½ teaspoon sugar
8 oz. (2 cups) strong plain (bread)
  flour

1 teaspoon salt
½ oz. (1 T) lard (shortening) or
  margarine
beaten egg or milk to glaze

Mix the fresh yeast with the warm water and sugar. Set aside until frothy.

Place the flour, salt and lard (shortening) or margarine in the mixer bowl and process until the mixture resembles breadcrumbs. With the motor running, pour the yeast liquid through the feed tube and process until the dough is well mixed. Remove the dough to an oiled bowl, cover with a damp cloth and leave in a warm place for 1 hour or until it has doubled in size.

Turn the dough onto a well-floured surface and flatten slightly Place the dough in the mixer bowl and process for a few seconds to knead it. Shape into an oblong and place in a greased 1 lb. loaf tin. Place in an oiled polythene (plastic) bag and leave to rise for 40 minutes or until the dough reaches the top of the tin.

Brush the dough with beaten egg or milk. Bake in a hot oven 450°F, Gas Mark 8 for 30-40 minutes or until it sounds hollow when tapped underneath. Cool on a wire rack.

Makes one 1 lb. loaf

RASPBERRY PANCAKES *(page 75)*
(Photograph: Stork Margarine)

DESSERTS

Cream Cherry Layer

USE THE DOUBLE-BLADED CHOPPING KNIFE.

6 oz. bread, crusts removed
2 oz. (¼ cup) butter
1 oz. (⅙ cup) demerara (raw)
  sugar
1 × 15 oz. can stoned (pitted)
  cherries, drained

½ pint (1¼ cups) thick cold custard
¼ pint (⅔ cup) double (heavy)
  cream
flaked almonds to decorate

Cut the bread into fingers. Place in the mixer bowl and process to
fine breadcrumbs.

Melt the butter in a saucepan, remove from the heat and stir in the
breadcrumbs and sugar. Allow to cool. Halve the cherries.

Place the custard and cream in the mixer bowl and process until
mixed. In 4 glasses make alternate layers of crumbs, cherries and
custard. Decorate with flaked almonds.
Serves 4

Banana Cream

USE THE DOUBLE-BLADED CHOPPING KNIFE.

3 ripe bananas
4 oz. (½ cup) sugar
juice of 1 lemon

½ pint (1¼ cups) double (heavy)
* cream*

Peel the bananas, place in the mixer bowl and process until smooth. Put the banana purée into a small saucepan with the sugar and lemon juice and bring to the boil, stirring. Leave to cool.

Whip the cream until it forms soft peaks. Fold the cream into the banana mixture and chill before serving.
Serves 4

Quick Strawberry Sorbet

USE THE DOUBLE-BLADED CHOPPING KNIFE.

1 lb. strawberries
juice of 1 orange
4 oz. (1 cup) icing (confectioners')
* sugar*

1 egg white, stiffly beaten

Place the strawberries, orange juice and sugar in the mixer bowl. Process until smooth. Pour the purée into a freezerproof container and freeze until slushy. Turn into the mixer bowl and process for 5 seconds. Add the beaten egg white and process for a further 2 seconds. Return to the container and freeze until just firm.
Serves 4

Raspberry Pancakes

USE THE DOUBLE-BLADED CHOPPING KNIFE.

2 oz. (½ cup) plain (all-purpose)
* flour*
¼ teaspoon salt
1 egg

¼ pint (⅔ cup) milk
oil for frying
1 lb. raspberries
2 dessert apples, cored and chopped

Place the flour, salt, egg and milk in the mixer bowl and process until the mixture is smooth. Use the batter to make 8 pancakes. Keep warm.

Divide the raspberries and apples between the pancakes and roll up.
Serves 4

Crispy Pineapple Meringue

USE THE DOUBLE-BLADED CHOPPING KNIFE.

2 teaspoons castor sugar
2 oz. (¼ cup) butter
6 slices white bread, crusts removed
1 × 16 oz. can pineapple chunks,
* drained and the juice reserved*

2 tablespoons cornflour (cornstarch)
1 oz. (2 T) sugar
juice of ½ lemon
2 eggs, separated
3 oz. (⅓ cup) castor sugar

Mix together the 2 teaspoons of sugar and the butter. Spread the bread on both sides with this mixture. Cut 5 of the slices into 3 fingers. Arrange the fingers close together around the sides of a deep 2½ pint (3 pint) ovenproof dish. Place the whole slice on the base, trimming the corners if necessary. Bake in a moderate oven, 350°F, Gas Mark 4 for 20 minutes until lightly browned.

Make up the pineapple juice to ½ pint (1¼ cups). Pour into a small saucepan and bring to the boil. Pour into the mixer bowl and add the cornflour (cornstarch), sugar, lemon juice and egg yolks. Process until smooth. Stir in the pineapple chunks and pour into the saucepan. Simmer for 2-3 minutes to thicken. Pour into the bread shell.

Whisk the egg whites until very stiff. Gradually add the sugar whisking well between each addition. Pile the meringue decoratively on top of the pineapple filling. Bake for a further 8-10 minutes or until the meringue is golden brown.

Serve hot.

Serves 4-6

CRISPY PINEAPPLE MERINGUE, CREAM CHERRY LAYER
(page 74), FRUITY CRUMB PUDDING *(page 78)*
(Photograph: Flour Advisory Bureau)

Fruity Crumb Pudding

USE THE DOUBLE-BLADED CHOPPING KNIFE.

4 slices white bread, crusts removed
4 oz. (1 cup) plain (all-purpose)
 flour
1 teaspoon baking powder
½ teaspoon salt
3 oz. (⅓ cup) castor sugar
3 oz. (⅝ cup) shredded suet

1 egg
8 tablespoons milk
3 oz. (½ cup) dried mixed fruit
Sauce:
3 tablespoons apricot jam
2 tablespoons sugar
4 tablespoons water

Grease a 2 pint (5 cup) pudding basin (steaming mold).

Place the bread in the mixer bowl and process to rough breadcrumbs. Add the flour, baking powder, salt, sugar, suet, egg and milk and process until mixed. Stir in the dried fruit. Pour the mixture into the pudding basin (mold), cover with foil and steam for 2½ hours or until cooked.

Place all the sauce ingredients in a small saucepan and slowly bring to the boil, stirring. Unmould the pudding onto a warm serving dish and serve with the sauce.
Serves 6

Chocolate and Raisin Pudding

USE THE DOUBLE-BLADED CHOPPING KNIFE.

4 oz. (½ cup) butter
4 oz. (½ cup) castor sugar
1 tablespoon cocoa powder
  (unsweetened)
2 tablespoons hot water
2 eggs

4 oz. (½ cup) self-raising flour
2 oz. (⅓ cup) raisins
Sauce:
4 oz. plain (semi-sweet) chocolate,
  melted

Grease 12 dariole moulds.

Place the butter and sugar in the mixer bowl and process until light and fluffy. Mix together the cocoa and water and, with the motor running, add to the butter mixture. Add the eggs, one at a time, processing after each addition. Turn off the motor, add the flour and process until just mixed. Stir in the raisins.

Divide the mixture between the dariole moulds, place them on a baking sheet and bake in a moderately hot oven, 375°F, Gas Mark 5 for 20-25 minutes or until a skewer inserted in the centre comes out clean.

Turn out the puddings onto a serving dish and pour over the melted chocolate.
Serves 6

Orange Topsy Turvy

USE THE DOUBLE-BLADED CHOPPING KNIFE.

4 oz. (1 cup) self-raising flour
1 teaspoon baking powder
4 oz. (½ cup) margarine, softened
4 oz. (½ cup) castor sugar
2 large eggs

grated rind of 1 orange
Topping:
3 tablespoons orange jelly
  marmalade
2 oranges, peeled, sliced and halved

Place the flour, baking powder, margarine, sugar, eggs and orange rind in the mixer bowl and process until the mixture is light and fluffy.

Spread the marmalade over the bottom of an 8 inch square cake tin. Arrange the orange slices over the marmalade and spoon the cake mixture on top.

Bake in a moderately hot oven, 375°F, Gas Mark 5 for 30-35 minutes or until golden brown and a skewer inserted in the centre comes out clean. Turn out the cake onto a serving dish and serve hot with custard.
Serves 4-6

Cherry and Almond Pudding

USE THE DOUBLE-BLADED CHOPPING KNIFE.

4 oz. (½ cup) butter
4 oz. (½ cup) castor sugar
2 eggs
4 oz. (½ cup) self-raising flour
few drops almond essence
1 × 15 oz. can stoned (pitted) red
  cherries, drained, and the juice
  reserved, and halved

Sauce:
4 tablespoons raspberry jam, sieved
juice from can of cherries
2 teaspoons cornflour (cornstarch)

Grease a 1½ pint (3¾ cup) pudding basin (steaming mold).
   Place the butter and sugar in the mixer bowl and process until light and fluffy. With the motor running add the eggs one at a time, processing after each addition. Switch off, add the flour and almond essence and process to mix. Stir in the cherries. Pour the mixture into the basin (mold), cover with foil and steam 1¼–1½ hours or until cooked through.
   In a saucepan heat the jam and cherry juice. Place the cornflour (cornstarch) in the mixer bowl pour in the sauce and process until mixed. Pour the mixture into the saucepan and simmer for 2–3 minutes.
   Unmould the pudding onto a warm serving dish and serve with the sauce.
Serves 4-6

Cherry Fool

USE THE DOUBLE-BLADED CHOPPING KNIFE.

8 oz. cherries, stoned (pitted)
¼ pint (⅔ cup) double (heavy)
  cream
3 oz. (6 T) castor sugar

1 teaspoon lemon juice
grated rind of ½ orange
cherries to decorate

Place the cherries, cream, sugar, juice and rind in the mixer bowl. Process until smooth. Pour the mixture into a serving dish and decorate with cherries.
Serves 4

CHERRY AND ALMOND PUDDING,
CHOCOLATE AND RAISIN PUDDING *(page 79)*,
ORANGE TOPSY TURVY *(page 79)*
(Photograph: Flour Advisory Bureau)

Chocolate Profiteroles

USE THE DOUBLE-BLADED CHOPPING KNIFE.

¼ pint (⅔ cup) water
2 oz. (¼ cup) margarine
2½ oz. (½ cup plus 2 T) flour
2 eggs

½ pint (1 ¼ cups) double (heavy) cream
4 oz. plain (semi-sweet) chocolate, melted

Place the water and margarine in a saucepan. Heat until the margarine has melted and the mixture comes to the boil.

Draw the pan to the side and pour in the sifted flour all at once. Beat vigorously with a wooden spoon until smooth. Transfer to the mixer bowl and process for 5 seconds. Add the eggs, one at a time, processing after each addition.

Either fill a large piping bag fitted with a large éclair nozzle with the dough and pipe shapes or drop teaspoons of the dough onto a wetted baking sheet. Bake in a hot oven, 425°F, Gas Mark 7 for 10-15 minutes. With a knife, slit the pastries to let out the steam, then return to the oven for a further 10-15 minutes to dry out. Cool on a wire rack.

Process the cream in the mixer bowl until thick. Fill each pastry with a little of the cream. Pile the filled pastries onto a serving dish and pour over the melted chocolate. Serve immediately.
Serves 4

DRINKS

Merry Widow Fizz

USE THE DOUBLE-BLADED CHOPPING KNIFE.

3 eggs
3 teaspoons castor sugar
juice of 1 small lemon

juice of 1 small orange
¼ pint (²/₃ cup) gin
soda water

Place the eggs, sugar, lemon and orange juices and the gin in the mixer bowl. Process until mixed.

Strain into 3 tall glasses and top up with soda water.
Serves 3

Cinnamon Coffee

USE THE DOUBLE-BLADED CHOPPING KNIFE.

½ pint (1¼ cups) strong sweetened
 black coffee
1 teaspoon ground cinnamon

1 pint (2½ cups) milk
1 teaspoon brandy
4 cinnamon sticks for serving

Heat the coffee. Place the ground cinnamon in the mixer bowl. Pour in the coffee and leave to stand for 10-15 minutes.

Add to the mixer bowl the milk and brandy. Process for a second and chill before serving. Pour into 4 glasses and serve with a cinnamon stick in each glass.
Serves 4

Hot Banana Whip

USE THE DOUBLE-BLADED CHOPPING KNIFE.

3 bananas
1 tablespoon lemon juice
1 1/2 pints (3 3/4 cups) milk

few drops vanilla essence
1 tablespoon icing (confectioners')
    sugar

Cut 8 thin slices of banana and sprinkle them with the lemon juice to prevent discoloration.

Heat the milk to just below boiling point. Pour into the mixer bowl and add the remaining bananas, vanilla essence and icing (confectioners') sugar. Process until smooth. Pour into 4 hot mugs and decorate with the banana slices.
Serves 4

Egg Flip

USE THE DOUBLE-BLADED CHOPPING KNIFE.

1 pint (2 1/2 cups) milk
4 eggs, separated
4 teaspoons castor sugar

4 tablespoons sherry
grated nutmeg

Heat the milk to just below boiling point.

Place the egg yolks, sugar and sherry in the mixer bowl, pour in the hot milk and process to mix.

Lightly whisk the egg whites by hand until frothy. Add to the mixer bowl and process until just mixed. Pour into 3 warm mugs or glasses and sprinkle a little nutmeg over the top of the liquid.
Serves 3

Yogurt Raspberry Cooler

USE THE DOUBLE-BLADED CHOPPING KNIFE.

1/2 pint (1 1/4 cups) raspberry yogurt
1 pint (2 1/2 cups) milk

4 teaspoons honey
2 oz. raspberries

Place the yogurt, milk, honey and raspberries in the mixer bowl, reserving a few raspberries for decoration. Process until smooth. Chill before serving. Pour cooler into tall glasses and decorate with a few of the reserved raspberries.

HOT BANANA WHIP, EGG FLIP, YOGURT RASPBERRY COOLER
CINNAMON COFFEE *(page 83)*, HAWAIIAN REFRESHER *(page 86)*
(Photograph: Unigate)

Hawaiian Refresher

USE THE DOUBLE-BLADED CHOPPING KNIFE.

1 large can pineapple cubes, drained
1½ pints (3¾ cups) milk
few drops yellow colouring
1 tablespoon rum essence

Decoration:
¼ pint (⅔ cup) double (heavy)
 cream
flaked chocolate

Place the pineapple cubes, milk, colouring and rum essence in the mixer bowl and process until smooth. Chill.

Process the cream in the mixer bowl until thick. Serve the drink in 4 tall glasses decorated with a spoonful of cream and a small piece of flaked chocolate.

Serves 4

Cardinal Cup

USE THE DOUBLE-BLADED CHOPPING KNIFE.

4 eggs
½ pint (1¼ cups) white wine
½ pint (1¼ cups) Burgundy

1 oz. (2T) castor sugar
juice of 2 oranges

Place in the mixer bowl the eggs, wines, sugar and orange juice. Process for a second and strain into 4 or 6 glasses.

Serves 4-6

Lemon Tea Nectar

USE THE DOUBLE-BLADED CHOPPING KNIFE.

¼ pint (⅔ cup) strong hot tea
2 strips lemon rind
2 teaspoons castor sugar

1 egg
1 teaspoon lemon juice
slice of lemon to decorate

In the mixer bowl pour the tea, lemon rind, sugar, egg and lemon juice. Process for a second. Strain into a glass and serve cold, decorated with the lemon slice.

Serves 1

Lime Frappé

USE THE DOUBLE-BLADED CHOPPING KNIFE.

2 small dessert apples, peeled and
  cored
2 eggs
¼ pint (⅔ cup) lime cordial
1½ tablespoons castor sugar
¼ pint (⅔ cup) water

6 drops almond essence
ice-cubes
soda water
apple slices dipped in lemon juice to
  decorate

Quarter the apples and place in the mixer bowl with the eggs, lime
cordial, sugar, water and essence. Process until smooth and strain
into 2 glasses. Add ice-cubes and top up with soda water. Decorate
with the apple slices.

Serves 2

Mocha Praline

USE THE DOUBLE-BLADED CHOPPING KNIFE.

4 oz. (½ cup) sugar
4 tablespoons water
2 oz. (½ cup) chopped hazelnuts
2 oz. (½ cup) chopped almonds
3 oz. plain (semi-sweet) chocolate,
  melted
2 oz. (½ cup) coffee powder

sugar to taste
¼ pint (⅔ cup) boiling water
1¼ pints (3 cups) milk, chilled
1-2 tablespoons brandy
¼ pint (⅔ cup) double (heavy)
  cream

Place the sugar and water in a small saucepan. Heat together until the
sugar has dissolved and then boil vigorously until the mixture turns
golden brown. Remove from the heat and add hazelnuts and
almonds and mix well. Spread on to an oiled piece of foil and leave
to harden. When cold, break into small pieces.

Place the melted chocolate, coffee powder, sugar to taste, and
boiling water in the mixer bowl. Process until the coffee powder has
dissolved.

Chill the mixture and stir in the milk and brandy. Process the
cream in the mixer bowl until thick.

Serve the chocolate mixture in 4 glasses and top with a spoonful of
cream and some of the crushed praline.

Serves 4

Cherry Ripe Zingers

USE THE DOUBLE-BLADED CHOPPING KNIFE.

8 oz. red or black cherries, stoned
 (pitted)
8 tablespoons maraschino juice
1 pint (2½ cups) milk

1 tablespoon cherry liqueur
¼ pint (⅔ cup) double (heavy)
 cream
4 cherries

Place the cherries, maraschino juice, milk, cherry liqueur in the mixer bowl and process to mix. Chill until ready to serve.
   Process the cream until thick. Serve the cherry mixture in 4 chilled glasses and top with a spoonful of cream and a cherry.
Serves 4

Minty Refresher

USE THE DOUBLE-BLADED CHOPPING KNIFE.

¼ pint (⅔ cup) double (heavy)
 cream
1½ pints (3¾ cups) milk
few drops peppermint essence

few drops green colouring
few drops Crème de Menthe
honey to taste
flaked chocolate to decorate

Place the cream in the mixer bowl and process until thick. Spoon into a small bowl.
   Pour the milk, peppermint essence, green colouring, Crème de Menthe and honey to taste in the mixer bowl. Process to mix. Chill until just before serving. Pour into 4 chilled glasses, and serve topped with a blob of whipped cream and a little flaked chocolate.
Serves 4

Taste of Honey

USE THE DOUBLE-BLADED CHOPPING KNIFE.

1½ pints (3¾ cups) milk
4 tablespoons honey

1 tablespoon rum

Heat the milk to just below boiling point. Pour into the mixer bowl and add the honey and rum. Process to mix and serve in 4 warm mugs or glasses.
Serves 4

CHERRY RIPE ZINGER, TASTE OF HONEY, MINTY
REFRESHER, MOCHA PRALINE *(page 87)*
COFFEE AND GINGER FRAPPÉ *(page 90) (Photograph: Unigate)*

Coffee and Ginger Frappé

USE THE DOUBLE-BLADED CHOPPING KNIFE.

2 oz. (½ cup) coffee powder
¼ pint (⅔ cup) boiling water
1½ pints (3¾ cups) milk
1½ oz. stem (preserved) ginger
3 tablespoons stem (preserved)
 ginger syrup from jar

Decoration:
¼ pint (⅔ cup) double (heavy)
 cream
a few coffee granules

Place the coffee powder, boiling water, milk, ginger and syrup into
the mixer bowl and process until the coffee has dissolved. Chill until
just before serving.
 Place the cream in the mixer bowl and process until thick.
 Serve the coffee frappé in 4 glasses and top with a spoonful of
cream sprinkled with a few coffee granules.
Serves 4

Prairie Oyster

USE THE DOUBLE-BLADED CHOPPING KNIFE.

3 tablespoons brandy
1 tablespoon Worcestershire sauce
2 teaspoons vinegar
1 teaspoon tomato ketchup

1 teaspoon Angostura bitters
1 egg yolk
pinch cayenne pepper

This drink is a classic morning-after-the-night-before reviver.
It should be swallowed in one gulp.
 Place the brandy, Worcestershire sauce, vinegar, tomato ketchup,
Angostura bitters, egg yolk and the cayenne pepper to taste in the
mixer bowl and process for a second. Pour into a glass.
Serves 1

INDEX

INDEX

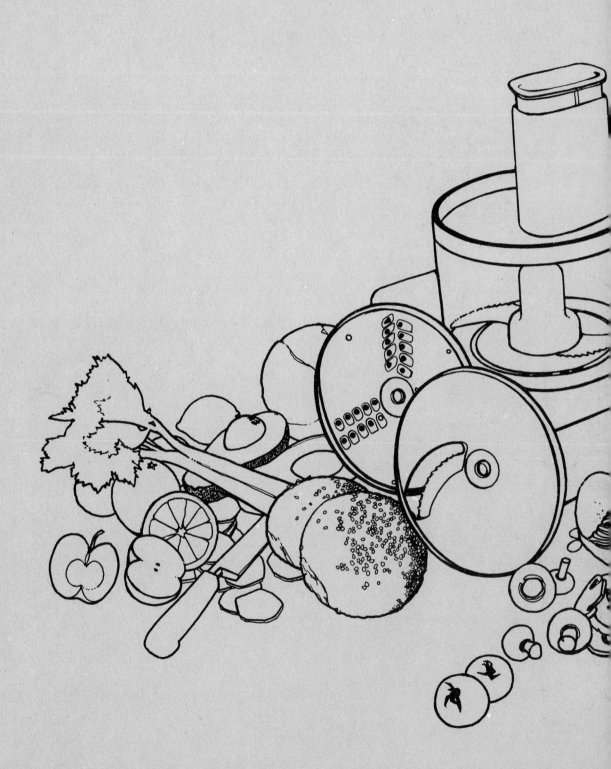